"In a day when positioning and posturing become surrogates for pastoring and Klout Score and creativity is proxy for Christ-likeness, someone needs to quell the tide by saying 'Enough!' That someone is Jonathan Martin who, through careful exegesis and crafted stories, asks us to lead at a higher level by developing, promoting and platforming the talents, gifts and passions of those around us. Humility and servanthood is still the hallmark of Christian leadership."

Eric Swanson
Leadership Network, Co-author of *The Externally Focused Church* and *To Transform a City*

Breaking the
King Saul Syndrome

The cancerous crown and its cure:

giving the kingdom away

Jonathan Martin

Portland, Oregon

BREAKING THE KING SAUL SYNDROME
The cancerous crown and its cure: giving the kingdom
away

Published in the USA by
Co-Serve International
P.O. Box 40567
Portland, OR 97240

ISBN 978-0-9847161-2-8

Edited by Daniel Ballast and Marshall Christensen
Cover design by Arnold Ramos

Printed in the USA

To my Dad – Trueman Million Martin Jr. (I love that name) but who is better known as Ted. I recently racked my brain and came up with about 10 men who exemplify the kind of leadership written about in this book. You were at the top of that list.

Contents

Foreword

The world is crying out for a different kind of leadership. These cries stretch from Wall Street to the streets of the Arab world. People are fed up with leaders who hold on to power so they can benefit themselves at the expense of their people.

We heard these cries when we started teaching leadership courses to young people at a university in Kazakhstan in 2004. Students were eager to talk about the leadership problems that they saw in the world and possible solutions. These experiences significantly shaped our mission as an organization to share truth across Eurasia by teaching the concepts of "servant leadership."

As we shared about our work with our Christian friends, somewhat to our surprise, they added their cries as well, by responding, "Servant leadership is what we need in our churches!" As it turns out, leadership in most churches looks very similar to leadership in the world.

Jesus, however, modeled something different – the way of leading by serving.

Jonathan Martin shows us that leading by serving is all about giving the Kingdom away.

This book, about the cancerous crown and its cure, is a personal challenge as well as a practical roadmap for leaders in the church – and the world.

It is time for radical surgery – cutting out the ways of the world and grafting in the Jesus model of servant leadership. We hope you will seriously consider Jonathan's challenge, and join those of us who are trying to walk down a different leadership path.

Marshall Christensen and Dan Ballast
Co-Serve International

Prologue

Several years ago I was asked to speak at a church retreat. I asked the pastor what he would like me to speak on. He gave me the reply I dread most. "You have free rein. Whatever you want."

"So what do I want? What should I speak on?" This question plagued me for several days. Then it came to me. Jonathan. That is my name, and I had never heard anyone speak on Jonathan. I would show up to speak dressed like King David and tell the story of his friendship with Jonathan.

I had no clue this seemingly small decision to become King David for a weekend would profoundly change my thinking and the course of my life and ministry.

I told the story in three fifty-minute sessions. The last one ended with David's lament after receiving the news concerning King Saul and his son

Jonathan: Their bodies lay lifeless on the slopes of Mt. Gilboa.

I stood in front of about 100 people at this weekend retreat.   But the people in the audience disappeared.   I was no longer acting, and in that moment I could see what David saw.   I could feel what David felt.   And I began weeping and sobbing almost uncontrollably.   Even now as I pen these words, tears overwhelm me.   He is dead.

As I stood there in the camp meeting room nearly three thousand years after the actual event, I still did not want to believe it. *Oh God, please no!! It can't be.* But it was true.   Jonathan lay dead.

Your glory, O Israel, lies slain on your heights.
How the mighty have fallen!

Tell it not in Gath,
proclaim it not in the streets of Ashkelon,
lest the daughters of the Philistines be glad,
lest the daughters of the uncircumcised rejoice.

O mountains of Gilboa,
may you have neither dew nor rain,
nor fields that yield offerings of grain.
For there the shield of the mighty was defiled,

the shield of Saul-no longer rubbed with oil.
From the blood of the slain,
from the flesh of the mighty,
the bow of Jonathan did not turn back,
the sword of Saul did not return unsatisfied.

Saul and Jonathan-
in life they were loved and gracious,
and in death they were not parted.
They were swifter than eagles,
they were stronger than lions.

O daughters of Israel,
weep for Saul,
who clothed you in scarlet and finery,
who adorned your garments with ornaments of gold.

How the mighty have fallen in battle!
Jonathan lies slain on your heights.
I grieve for you, Jonathan my brother;
you were very dear to me.
Your love for me was wonderful,
more wonderful than that of women.

How the mighty have fallen!
The weapons of war have perished!

2 Samuel 1:19-27 (NIV)

I don't know if my presentation affected anyone there that day – but I was changed. The sorrow I felt as I, David, wept for a friend unlike any other in history. A friend unmatched in literature.

Would anyone weep for me the way David did for Jonathan? I feared not. I had never given my all for a friend like Jonathan did. He gave away his life, his crown, his kingdom – everything he had and was.

I left that camp determined to be like Jonathan. To be like the man my father and mother had named me after.

Father in Heaven, may I be like Jonathan, and give your Kingdom away.

Jonathan Martin
June 2, 2009

Oh, How the Mighty Have Fallen!

Two men. Father and Son. King and Prince. Both Warriors. Both regal in stature and appearance. Both slain on the rounded gentle slopes of Mt. Gilboa. To the victorious Philistines the only difference in these men was their age. But to God, and to God's anointed – David – the contrast could not have been greater.

Two men. One – an enemy who could not sleep until David was dead. One – a friend who would give all he had so that David would be all he could be.

Two men. One – possessed with a self-consuming and all controlling pride. One – possessed with an inexplicable humility unequaled in secular literature and history.

Two men. One – an enemy of God and his Kingdom. One – a friend of God and committed to his Kingdom no matter the personal sacrifice.

Two men. One – corrupted by the love and need for power. One – committed to empowering others.

Two men. One – obsessed with his need to control. One – realizing God is in control.

They both lay dead. Side by side. There could not be a greater contrast in men. "Oh how the mighty have fallen."

Saul – with a fall like Lucifer's in every respect.

Jonathan – like Jesus in so many ways.

> *They both lay dead. Side by side. There could not be a greater contrast in men.*

There lay King Saul disgraced, pathetically clutching his crown.

And there lay his son Jonathan full of grace, hands generously open, having given his crown – having given the Kingdom away.

However, in a sense, King Saul did not die that day. The very things that drove King Saul to personal shame and disgrace still drive and control many leaders. Christian leaders. Anyone who aspires to leadership, and even those who have leadership thrust upon them, will be hounded by the specter of King Saul who sought to hold on to his power at all costs. And indeed, it cost him all.

I call it the *King Saul Syndrome.* Every Christian leader comes face to face with it. I have too often seen it in myself. If you will take the time to read this short book, you will see the fertile seeds of the syndrome in yourself. Many are taken over by its power and destroyed. Some – way too few – know the joys of living free from its effects. Jonathan was one of those chosen few. I, the Jonathan writing this book, have just begun to taste this freedom from the control of the King Saul Syndrome. The small taste I have had makes me want to share it with the world.

The Cancerous Crown
The Fall of the House of Saul

Power is my mistress. I have worked too hard at her conquest to allow anyone to take her away from me.
Napoleon

Saul's fall did not start with himself – though no doubt the potential was there. It started with the cry of the people. "Give us a king!   Give us a king like the rest of the people."   People everywhere want a king. They cry out for a figurehead – a powerful leader.   And that is not necessarily a good thing. Look what the prophet Samuel had to say to their request:

> And Samuel said to the sons of Israel, "Thus says the Lord, the God of Israel, 'I brought Israel up from Egypt, and I delivered you from the hand of the Egyptians, and from the power of all the kingdoms that were oppressing you.' But you

today rejected your God, who delivers you from all your calamities and your distresses; yet you have said, 'No, but set a king over us!' Now therefore, present yourselves before the Lord by your tribes and by your clans."
(1 Samuel 10:17-19)

So, this desire to have an earthly king is not a good thing. Couple this with man's lust for power, and we have a volatile combination.

Samuel makes sure the people know what this choice for a king means:

> *So, this desire to have a king is not a good thing. Couple this with man's lust for power, and we have a volatile combination.*

So Samuel spoke all the words of the Lord to the people who had asked of him a king. And he said, "This will be the procedure of the king who will reign over you: he will take your sons and place them for himself in his chariots and among his horsemen and they will run before his chariots. And he will appoint for himself commanders of thousands and of fifties, and

some to do his plowing and to reap his harvest and to make his weapons of war and equipment for his chariots. He will also take your daughters for perfumers and cooks and bakers. And he will take the best of your fields and your vineyards and your olive groves, and give them to his servants. And he will take a tenth of your seed and of your vineyards, and give to his officers and to his servants. He will also take your male servants and your female servants and your best young men and your donkeys, and use them for his work. He will take a tenth of your flocks, and you yourselves will become his servants. Then you will cry out in that day because of your king whom you have chosen for yourselves, but the Lord will not answer you in that day." *Nevertheless, the people refused to listen to the voice of Samuel, and they said, "No, but there shall be a king over us...."*
(1 Samuel 8:10-19)

They just would not listen. Saul didn't seem to be seeking this position of power. The kingship was thrust upon him.

Saul's Humble Beginnings

A donkey chaser. When we first meet Saul in 1 Samuel 9 and 10, he was looking for lost donkeys. It didn't seem to be the noblest of callings.

Hiding in the baggage. In 1 Samuel 10:17-27, when Saul's glorious moment had arrived and he was to be announced as the first king of Israel, he hid in the baggage. Saul was humble, shy and self-effacing. God had clearly chosen him. It had not been Saul who desired the power of being king.

The Beginning of the Syndrome

But then Saul became king and that changed everything.

In 1 Samuel 11 Saul wins a battle in the Holy Spirit's power. The people see him as an amazing warrior. They speak of his greatness. And though at first he gives credit where credit is due, Saul starts to believe their words. He really is something. He becomes proud. The kingdom suddenly becomes about him and not really about the kingdom at all.

What about the God who got him here and the Holy Spirit who empowered him? Yes, it was kind for God to play a role. But it sure feels good to be somebody of such grand significance: to be king over God's Kingdom. Now that is some kind of power!

Overstepping His Role

If being king was not honor enough, how about being a prophet and priest as well? Saul knew it was Samuel's job to offer the sacrifices, but because of extenuating circumstances we see Saul in 1 Samuel 13 taking over the role of prophet and priest as well. His men were scattering. He had to take control. If he failed to step up and perform the sacrifice, he would look weak in front of all the people. They might think he was dependent on Samuel to get the job done. Since when did any king need to wait on others? This simply did not appear "kingly." Saul had to step up and be the man. He took the lead.

But in actuality, he gave up his right to lead.

Disobeying God

Saul refuses to totally destroy the Amalekites as God had commanded. God grants him the victory and he sets up a monument to himself. He not only disobeys God but flaunts his stuff. God is not impressed. The prophet Samuel reprimands Saul in 1 Samuel 15 and tells him:

> Is it not true, though you were little in your own eyes, you were made the head of the tribes of Israel? And the LORD anointed you king over Israel. . . . Why then did you not obey the voice of the LORD, but rushed upon the spoil and did what was evil in the sight of the LORD?
> (1 Samuel 15:17,19)

Then after Saul argues that he did indeed obey, but simply kept the animals to sacrifice to Samuel's God, Samuel delivers these famous lines:

> Has the LORD as much delight in burnt offerings and sacrifices as in obeying the voice of the LORD? Behold, to obey is better than sacrifice, and to heed than the fat of rams.

For rebellion is as the sin of divination, and insubordination is as iniquity and idolatry. Because you have rejected the word of the LORD, he has also rejected you from being king.
(1 Samuel 15:22-23)

Apparently Saul did not agree – not when obedience would have dropped his popularity rating through the floor. After all, allowing his men to take the plunder made perfect sense. They had worked hard and sacrificed for this victory. Why would anyone want to burn the loot? Saul demonstrated his belief that leading is largely about staying popular. It was important for Saul to be liked, especially by the army who kept him in power. People tend to follow those they like, and are more prone to rebel against those they don't. Saul "feared the people" rather than God and caved in under this pressure – and God declared that the kingdom was now stripped from him.

Fighting against God

From the moment of this disobedience until the end of his life Saul fought against God – he was determined to hold on to the kingdom that God had given away to another, namely David. I am sure Saul "meant well" by waging war against God, but fighting against the Almighty is not the brightest idea.

Saul tried to hold on to power at all costs. Holding on to power is not easy, especially when someone younger is showing you up at every turn. And it gets really difficult when the Holy Spirit is clearly with the younger guy. King Saul felt there was only one option. Get rid of David. Kill the one whose very presence challenged his authority. "No person should like anyone better than their own king. I, the king, alone should be the national hero. God knew what he was doing when he brought me to power – so I need to make sure that I stay in power. I remember well the day I was anointed king. So king I will stay – no matter the cost."

So that reign which began in humility, ended on the slopes of Mt. Gilboa in humiliation. Begging his armor bearer to end his life, a cowardly old man died shamefully, pathetically clutching his crown – a crown that was never his in the first place.

But the story is not over.

Saul's story continues today in church after church, in ministry after ministry, in business after business, in virtually every political office, on every continent and in every country. The King Saul Syndrome grabs hold of leader after leader, over and over and over again.

I know a man who is gifted in speech, in relationships and in teaching. He is sharp witted and a talented musician. He's a good evangelist. He was asked to be the pastor in the small community where he had grown up.

> *Power is something of which I am convinced there is no innocence this side of the womb.*
> **Nadine Gordimer**

Being the most gifted speaker in the church, he naturally did all the speaking. Being a professional musician, he featured there as well. Being gifted in all ways, people naturally loved him. They had gotten their king – oh sorry – I mean, pastor.

I will call him Pastor Stan. The church grew amazingly under Pastor Stan. The church became known as "Pastor Stan's Church." I'm sure Pastor Stan wanted the best for the community, but over time the best for the community somehow came to mean – him.

The church had a desire to go deeper in the word, and so on Wednesday nights a Bible scholar from another community was brought in. People loved this. When this man finished his 10 weeks people wanted this kind of teaching to continue. Dr. Searson, a member of the church, volunteered to do a series. It was so popular that the Wednesday night teaching time grew and people started saying Dr. Searson should be given a chance to preach.

He was not allowed to preach. In fact, Pastor Stan insisted that instead of Dr. Searson, Pastor Stan himself would take over the Wednesday night teaching. Now Pastor Stan was preaching three times on Sunday, always in the community, doing music and teaching Wednesday night as well (with Dr. Searson effectively silenced). Soon Pastor Stan's family and health began to suffer.

He was diagnosed with a condition and his family and marriage were in such a state that it was clear he should step down from being the pastor.

But he was God's anointed leader! He had been and believed he was still called to this church. He rallied those closest to him and the fight to keep his unraveling kingdom began.

It destroyed the church.

He attacked friends who tried to talk sense to him. His best friends and leaders were forced to scatter. He alienated his wife and kids. He wrecked all he had lived for. There he lay bleeding on the slopes of Mt. Gilboa. "Oh how the mighty have fallen." Stan went down clutching his crown. A crown that was never his in the first place. He should have given the Kingdom away.

Pastor Stan started off humbly. Then he overstepped his bounds. He sacrificed and worked harder when he saw the potential for loss of power and position. He tried to keep power at all costs. And how it cost him. Everything.

If only Stan had seen that everyone in the church was anointed of God for ministry. They were anointed in some way, perhaps to teach, to do music, to reach into the community, to preach or to evangelize. He should have given the kingdom to each person. He would not have burned out and pride would not have had the same chance to turn him into just another casualty – of the King Saul Syndrome.

Pastor and ministry leader meltdown and burnout are huge because King Saul still lives. Yet there is an answer. It is found in the rest of the story. This part is about a man who is often forgotten. Simply not noticed. Passed by. Looked over. His name is Jonathan – the man who would *not* be king.

The Cure

Jonathan: the man who would NOT be king

I hope our wisdom will grow with our power, and teach us, that the less we use our power the greater it will be.

Thomas Jefferson

This is one story where we cannot use the old adage: Like father – like son. Oh, Saul and Jonathan were probably both tall. They were both amazing men of war. But they were nothing alike.

Jonathan was next in line to be king. He had all the makings of a king – royal birth, height, stature, good looks, and he was an amazing warrior. He was a leader. He alone changed the whole course of a battle as he climbed the cliffs with his armor bearer to take out a Philistine garrison guarding the pass. When all others were hiding and cowering in holes, Jonathan took a stand against all odds, which turned the tide of the war and led to a great Israeli victory. Jonathan was perhaps the greatest warrior in Israel. Yes, Jonathan was fit to be king.

But something happened by the brook in the valley of Elah that would mark Jonathan for the rest of his life: The thundering contrabass voice of a Philistine giant defied the armies of the Living God.

Was there no leader to step up? Why didn't King Saul step forward to fight? Well, frankly he was getting a bit old. And the Holy Spirit – his power for victory – had been removed.

So who would you expect to step up to fight this uncircumcised giant? Jonathan. But where was he?

So who would you expect to step up to fight this uncircumcised giant?

Jonathan.

Jonathan, first in line for the throne and a warrior prince, is the most capable to stand up. But Jonathan is conspicuously absent. Where is he?

We can only conjecture, but there are not many options. Perhaps Saul, wanting to keep the throne even after his own death, stopped Jonathan. Some think Saul even put Jonathan under house arrest, knowing he was heir and next to be king.

Perhaps Jonathan was fearful and unable to trust the Lord in this situation.

What we do know is that he was there in the camp and yet he did not come forward. But another did.

As I imagine it, I can picture Jonathan's look of astonishment as he sees young David - *at least fifteen years his younger[1]* - saying he will stand up to Goliath. He's amazed at the young man's courage but is certain he will be killed. He recognizes David as the young musician who played for his father during his fits of madness. I imagine Jonathan

---

[1] Saul's son Ish-Bosheth was forty (2 Samuel 2:10) at the same time David was 30 (2 Samuel 5:4). There were other brothers, Abinadab and Malchi-shua (1 Samuel 31:2) between Jonathan and him. Saul was 72 at his death so Jonathan likely was 44 to 50 years old. A rough guess would be a 14-20 year difference, which makes the friendship all the more remarkable. David was not "an equal" even in age but treated by Jonathan as one even greater than himself with the love of a true friend. Friendships were meant to cross generational lines.

watching David as Saul tries to put his own armor on the untrained boy. I picture Jonathan's expression as this young lad decides to take the giant on without any armor at all. What a horrible waste of a young man's life – but Jonathan stands amazed at such principle and bravery. Jonathan watches David as he leaves the king's presence - his only protection being the Lord his God. I can see Jonathan as he makes his way to the battlefront and watches the drama unfold from the front lines. This boy steps out from the line of soldiers and walks down the ridge to cross the brook to meet Goliath. Jonathan's heart quickens as the giant's booming voice echoes, shaking the valley and every Israeli soldier as he mocks the young man less than one-quarter his size.

And then Jonathan hears David's declaration of faith:

> This day the Lord will deliver you up into my hands, and I will strike you down and remove your head from you. And I will give the dead bodies of the army of the Philistines this day to the birds of the sky and the wild beasts of the earth, that all the earth may know that there is a God in Israel and that all this assembly may

know that the Lord does not deliver by sword or by spear; for the battle is the Lord's and He will give you into our hands. (1 Samuel 17:46-47)

I imagine Jonathan's face as he watches the Philistine march and then run toward David. Then David, unbelievably, runs toward the giant. Jonathan clenches his fists and grits his teeth, grimacing and squinting, almost closing his eyes as he half turns his head away, afraid to watch, yet unwilling to miss what might happen. He watches the sling loose its single stone. And passes the longest half second of his life.

He hears the sickening thud, and watches with his jaw dropped as the giant comes crashing to the earth.

Silence. Astonishment. Awe.

The still air is shattered by thunderous shouts of victory as David takes the sword and finalizes the death of the enemy of God.

Jonathan is stunned.

He is left pondering and contemplating the meaning of all this. The Holy Spirit is clearly upon this young man - David.   This is absolutely undeniable.

Later Saul calls David in and speaks with him. Jonathan, watching and listening, is not moved toward pride, envy or jealousy – like any "mere man" would have been. Instead he is moved to respect and even love.   Here was a young man more than fifteen years his younger and yet Jonathan would see to it that this young man would become all that God had for

> *Jonathan, watching and listening, is not moved toward pride, envy or jealousy – like any other man would have been. Instead he is moved to love.*

him.   He would make sure David would become complete.   After the others had left that place, Jonathan made a covenant with the young man.

Jonathan took his princely robe and clothed David with it along with his own armor, his sword, his bow and his belt. In a symbolic gesture Jonathan was making this clear statement: *"Anything I have is yours.   I am committed to seeing you become everything God intends. I give the kingdom to you."*

The scriptures say that Jonathan loved David as himself. He laid down his right to the throne, his right to reign, and on that memorable day Jonathan acknowledged that God was in this young man.   There

> *Power is not alluring to pure minds.*
> **Thomas Jefferson.**

in the valley of Elah, Jonathan let go of his crown and gave the Kingdom away.

The Rock – A second look at 1 Samuel 20

Read the story. I remember hearing this story in Sunday school as a child. The teacher said this was David's plan to see what was in heart of King Saul. The teacher was wrong. As I recently reread the story, it was so clear that this was David's plan to see what was in the heart of Jonathan – the man he so wanted to believe was his friend.

David lay hidden in the field by the rock called Ezel. Every little sound set him on edge. A hare rushing through the grass. A fox bounding on the field mice. The mere rustling of the grass in the breeze. Every sound could be Saul and his soldiers coming to end his life.

The question in David's mind wasn't whether or not it was safe for him to return into the presence of King Saul. Saul had just tried to pin him to the wall with his spear. He knew Saul wanted him dead. The question that plagued David was this: "Will Jonathan turn on me? Will he send the soldiers to end my life? Will he try to lure me back into the king's presence so Saul can kill me? Or will he, against all odds, remain my true friend?"

David already knew Saul was not safe, but more than anything he wanted to believe that Jonathan was.

Listen to David's parting words to Jonathan before hiding in the field of Ezel:

> Therefore deal kindly with your servant, for you have brought your servant into a covenant of the LORD with you. But if there is iniquity in me, put me to death yourself; for why then should you bring me to your father? (1 Samuel 20:8)

And in response to these words Jonathan made another covenant with David.

> You shall remain by the stone Ezel. And I will shoot three arrows to the side, as though I shot at a target. And behold, I will send the lad, saying, "Go, find the arrows." If I specifically say to the lad, "Behold, the arrows are on this side of you, get them," then come; for there is safety for you and no harm, as the LORD lives. But if I say to the youth, "Behold, the arrows are beyond you," go, for the LORD has sent you away. As for the agreement of which you and I have spoken, behold, the LORD is between you and me forever." (1 Samuel 20:19-23)

So the covenant was made. But humanly speaking, this covenant made no sense for Jonathan to keep.

As David hid in the field, he must have realized it made more sense for Jonathan to break this covenant than to keep it.

Jonathan had every right culturally and biblically to stand by his father; to honor his father as the law commanded, and to honor his family as the culture demanded. For him to dishonor both his father and family clearly would leave him in cultural disgrace. It would also endanger Jonathan's own life as he would be declared a traitor – an enemy of the kingdom.

But even more significantly, David clearly knew he alone was the one who stood between Jonathan and the throne of Israel. Saul knew this. Jonathan knew this. History is populated with those who scheme to take

So the covenant was made. But humanly speaking, this covenant made no sense for Jonathan to keep.

power, who fight their way to the top, who kill to obtain power, and who murder to keep the throne.

Fear of a likely betrayal seized David's heart as he waited in the grass. Yet with that constant fear there was mingled a faint but living hope – that Jonathan would utterly deny himself, his family, and his right to reign on the throne, for a friend.

The morning of truth finally comes. Jonathan appears like he said he would. He is alone with just a lad, just like he had promised. Jonathan shoots the arrows. The lad runs after them. David's heart pounds as he waits to hear the shouts of the one who has been the truest of friends.

"*Is not the arrow beyond you? Hurry, be quick. Do not stay.*" (1 Samuel 20:37-38)

David was overwhelmed with emotion. His face fills with tears: "When the lad was gone, David rose from the south side and fell on his face to the ground, and bowed three times. And they kissed each other and wept together, but David more." (1 Samuel 20:41)

Then the older, more experienced man, turned to the youthful David and said, "Go in safety, inasmuch as we have sworn to each other in the name of the LORD, saying, 'The LORD will be between me and you, and between my descendants and your descendants forever.'" (1 Samuel 20:42)

They both arose and sorrowfully parted ways.

What kind of man was Jonathan? Listen to his father's words:

You're a son of a perverse and rebellious woman. Do I not know that you are choosing the son of Jesse to your own shame and to the shame of your mother's nakedness? For as long as the son of Jesse lives on the earth, neither you nor your kingdom will be established. (1 Samuel 20:31-31)

Jonathan knew this, yet he gave the Kingdom away.

Later as David and his band flee from Saul, Jonathan risks his own life by coming to David's hideout on Horesh. Jonathan well knew David's men would have every reason to view him – the king's son and heir – as an enemy to be feared and killed. And David, humanly speaking, would have cause to fear as well. Could Jonathan have had a change of mind?

And there Jonathan encouraged David in God. (1 Samuel 23:16). This friendship was about God, not two men. I imagine them around the campfire reliving and telling the stories of their times together, laughing and crying. David playing the harp and singing the songs Jonathan so much loved to hear. Jonathan reminding David to remain true to the One who had called him.

At Horesh Jonathan spoke the last words David would hear come from his lips: "Do not be afraid, because the hand of Saul my father shall not find you, and you will be king over Israel and I will be next to you; and Saul my father knows that also. So the two of them made a covenant before the LORD." (1 Samuel 23:17-18)

I wish I could have been by that fire. As David watched his friend leave, the last time he would see this man on the earth, he must have asked, "What kind of friend is this – who gives the Kingdom away?"

And the answer? The Bible makes it clear. Every believer is to be that kind of friend. It is the task of every leader – to want what God wants for the people they lead and minister to. It is the call of every follower of Jesus – to want what God wants for every friend. This is who Jesus is. He is the one who makes it possible for us to give ourselves and the Kingdom away.

The King Saul Syndrome:
It's Saul over this World

Where love rules, there is no will to power; and where power predominates, there love is lacking. The one is the shadow of the other.

Carl Jung

The attempt to combine wisdom and power has only rarely been successful and then only for a short while.

Albert Einstein

I had the amazing opportunity to work with many of the bishops in Sudan as our church and a couple of other American churches partnered to bring them all together for a consultation. One of the greatest parts of that trip was going and teaching with my father.

I felt compelled to warn them against the King Saul Syndrome for in the past many of these denominations had been competing for territory and their own little kingdoms. Now with the war on the South just ending, they were ready to work together.

The way I introduced the topic was to have my dad come up to the front of the room to sit on his throne. I called him the "chief." My 75 year old father really acted the part and the thirty plus leaders in the room smiled and laughed as my dad crossed his arms, furrowed his brow and frowned with a look of superiority.

> *Whom the gods would destroy, they first make mad with power.*
> **Charles Beard**

I introduced myself as his son. My dad got up and patted me on the head and then put me to the right of his throne and made me stand there.

I explained we were the best warriors in the whole tribe. We had been elevated to greatness because of our great abilities and wisdom. *My dad never stopped hamming it up – acting on my every description.*

But then something happened – the story continued. After a great battle, there arose a new hero. *I had one of the younger bishops stand up to act the part.* He not only saved the tribe once, but twice. And soon everyone was talking about him. They stopped talking about the greatness of the chief and his son. *As I narrated, the Sudanese bishop acting as the new hero was even a bigger ham than my dad.*

I looked at my dad. I looked at myself. We looked at each other. And then we turned and looked over at this new hero.

What should we – the chief and his son – do with this new hero? I asked the crowd.

The bishops' answer came back more quickly than my own echo.

"Kill him!"

Now, of course, they were not saying that this is the right answer. They were simply answering the way their people and all leaders around the world have answered ever since the creation of man. **"Kill him!"** He is a threat to power.

But fortunately this does not happen in the church – or does it? Here are some quick stories from around the world.

Kent came to Christ in his late twenties. He radically changed and was ready to reach others who had never heard of Jesus and his life changing power. Immediately he started attending the church closest to home. The pastor was delighted to have him added to the small congregation. Kent started attending a Bible college and started leading his neighbors to the Lord. The small church started to grow as family after family came to Christ. The pastor liked this and Kent, with the pastor's permission, started teaching a Sunday school class that would meet at nine. The pastor had been teaching the class and let Kent take it for a couple of months. As soon as Kent started teaching, the class mushroomed and tripled in size.

After many requests to allow Kent to continue to teach, the pastor decided to restart his own class at the same time as Kent's. Almost everyone wanted to go to Kent's class.

The pastor was faced with a choice. Like Jonathan, he could hand the Kingdom away by attending Kent's class and empowering him to become even better, or he could clutch his crown like King Saul. His decision became evident quickly.

"Kill him!"

The pastor began to accuse Kent of all kinds of immorality, spread rumors about him and finally kicked him out of the church. Kent had no clue what had just happened and sought reconciliation. But when Kent brought the leadership from his Bible college to help work through reconciliation between him and the pastor, the pastor refused to even meet.

One of the professors discerned that this pastor was enslaved to strong bitterness and predicted he would not live long unless he could let go of this all controlling jealousy. Within a year the pastor died of cancer. While on his deathbed he still spewed hatred toward Kent – falsely accusing him.

I know Kent today. He is one of the most amazing "Jonathan" types of servant leaders. He learned from this incident and from the scriptures what not to be. He is busy giving the Kingdom away working both with children and in missions overseas.

Guillermo was busy teaching and training Christian leaders in Latin America. They were all part of a large Christian organization and most upon graduation would be released back into this organization for ministry. Guillermo taught them "Jonathan" style leadership. *"Your primary job is to equip and train those you lead to be complete in Christ – to unleash them in the power and gifting of the Holy Spirit. It is not to command and control, but to empower – even if that means letting them surpass you."*

The problem was that once they got out of Guillermo's class and back into the Christian organization, they realized their own leader's style was "command and control." That was his culture's style of leadership and so he led that way, too.

"What do we do if our leader is not the kind of leader you told us about?" the recent graduates asked Guillermo.

The leader caught wind of this new "Jonathan" teaching. He had a choice. Clutch his crown or give the Kingdom away.

"Kill him!"

Guillermo was fired and asked to leave the country. The regional leader saw such teaching as a threat to his command and control style. He canned not only this teaching, but also the teacher.

Europe

In an eastern European country there is a pastor who is the head of the largest evangelical denomination in the country. One of the only growing churches organized a Christmas outreach concert in a small town 35 minutes south of this pastor's city. There is no church in this city, just one believer who has a heart for the lost in her village. When this pastor heard of this he called the church doing outreach in a rage and said, "What business is it of yours to be doing an outreach in 'our' territory. You have no right to evangelize in this city." On another occasion a young Bible school graduate and his wife moved into a city with no church just across the border. They felt led of the Lord to start a small Bible study in their home. When this pastor learned that there was a new group meeting 40 minutes from his town, he angrily called the leader and told him that he needs to get permission from him first. This same pastor leads the largest church in the country, but never has small groups because "people will talk to one another and then they will lead a revolt." These were his own words. So...

"Kill them!" before anyone else even has a chance to lead.

So this pastor leads nearly every gathering in the church. His kingdom is nicely controlled and tightly capped.

Africa

In a certain valley in Africa, some young men wanted to see the Kingdom grow. They began meeting in houses during the week for fellowship. These house fellowships began to grow and grow. More people went to these fellowships than attended the official services in the denomination's church buildings.

The local and older leaders of the church were being shown up. But what should they do? They could give the Kingdom away or clutch their crowns.

"Kill them!"

The house fellowships continued to grow. One evening some of the leaders in one of the house fellowships decided to serve communion. This brought an all out attack on the movement. You had to be ordained in order to offer the Eucharist, and these fellowship leaders were not ordained. The church leaders clamped down and killed the growing house fellowship movement.

In every continent, every country, every corner of this earth - King Saul is there. He is tragically trying to hang on to every tiny kingdom created in the vanity of man's frail and misguided heart. King Saul's specter lives. Too many good men[2] have been seduced and led to the grave by the powerful spirit of this deadly syndrome. Enough is enough. Yes, it's

---

[2] The term "men" is often used generically in this book to refer to church leaders. Both men and women can be in leadership roles that subject them to the King Saul Syndrome.

Saul over the world - but it is time we give Jesus the lead.

The Hunger to Lead:
The Seeds of the Syndrome

It is said that power corrupts, but actually it's more true that power attracts the corruptible. The sane are usually attracted by other things than power.
David Brin

"....do not take the place of honor, lest someone more distinguished than you may have been invited by him, and he who invited you both shall come and say to you, 'Give place to this man,' and then in disgrace you proceed to occupy the last place."
Jesus

Leadership is a hot topic. I Googled the word. In approximately .11 seconds it came up with 153,000,000 uses. Everywhere I turn, "Have you read so and so's book on leadership? You've got to."

So many aspire to lead. To be a leader. To be **the** leader.

Why lead? What is the big draw anyway?

I was preaching last weekend and so I just threw that question out there to the congregation. Here were the answers shouted back to me from the congregation:

- Ego
- Significance
- Power
- Influence
- Control

Instead of being told what to do, getting to tell others what to do. Getting things done your way.

They weren't particularly the Christian answers I wanted to hear. But they are the reasons we want to lead. But here is another reason we wish to lead. This one I came up with myself: *Instead of being used by others to help them fulfill their dream, as a leader I get to use others to help me fulfill mine.*

That last one sounds ugly. Use others? You may wonder how I came up with it. Unfortunately, it was not very hard. It came way too easily.

I went to Amazon.com and typed in "leadership." Out came several thousand titles. Here was the number one: *The 21 Irrefutable Laws of Leadership: Follow them and people will follow you.*

Implicit in that title is the idea that leadership is somehow about having people follow you. That makes sense. Doesn't it?

Just recently, the new Vice President Joe Biden told of a time he confronted former President George W. Bush. "I remember President Bush saying to me one time in the Oval Office," Biden began, "'Well, Joe,' he said, 'I'm a leader.' And I said: 'Mr. President, turn around and look behind you. No one is following.'"

Though many call this recollection of Biden's to be "creative" it still makes the point that leaders are leaders only if they are followed. How effective are you as a leader?

Well, how many are following? That just seems to be the logical question to ask. It seems as though "leader" and "follower" are inexorably linked.

Inseparable. No one following? – then to put it in the vernacular – you aint no leader!

First was Google. Then I went to Amazon.com. Well, I was on a technological roll. Typing leader and leadership into everything and seeing what it spit out.

Wait... Jesus. I had yet to type the word leader into my Bible software concordance to see what Jesus had to say.

L – E – A – D – E – R. There I typed it.

153,000,000 for Google.
334,558 for Amazon.com.
2 for Jesus. Two????

What did Jesus say about leadership? Here it is: "And do not be called leaders; for One is your Leader, that is, Christ. But the greatest among you shall be your servant. And whoever exalts himself shall be humbled; and whoever humbles himself shall be exalted." (Matthew 23:10-12)

What is Jesus saying? Don't be called leaders? This goes in the face of everything I have ever been taught. We humans are supposed to aspire to lead. We have one leader? – Christ? So we are not to pursue leadership? Instead we are to serve? Servanthood? Jesus has this way of standing everything on its head.

Could he possibly be saying that the goal of life is not to have people following us, but rather to serve in such a way that people would follow Christ?

So what else did Jesus have to say about leadership?

> And there arose also a dispute among them as to which one of them was regarded to be greatest. And He said to them, "The kings of the Gentiles lord it over them; and those who have authority over them are called 'Benefactors.' But not so with you, but let him who is the greatest among you become as the youngest, and the leader as the servant. (Luke 22:24-26)

The disciples were arguing over who was the top leader. They had it upside down.

A "benefactor" is not to be the one who benefits from those who are under him. Jesus reminds us that we are the ones who are to benefit others.

The King Saul Syndrome began in Saul after he became king. But it begins in us in our very aspiration to lead. To be the respected one. To be the guy on top. To be "the man." To be called "leader." To be called by any title at all – whether it be pastor, father, reverend, Dr., CEO, chairman, president, or king.

If we are seeking the crown in the first place, what is going to keep us from desperately trying to hold on to it once we have it? How likely will we be to want to give it away?

So our definitions:

Leader: *One who has others following.*

Servant: *One who works for the benefit of another.*

So according to these definitions, let's look at a few biblical heroes and see what kind of leaders they were.

John the Baptist: He had a following. People came from everywhere. He had disciples. He was "the man." Then something happened. Another man came onto the scene. The masses stopped coming around. They started to leave John to follow this other man. Even his closest disciples started leaving.

That had to hurt – your younger cousin showing you up. Those you love leaving you.

"He must increase, and I must decrease," John the Baptist said.

He understood, just like the man Jonathan whose name he shared. It was not about being followed but about getting people to follow Jesus. John sat alone in prison. No one followed him anymore.

So by our world's definitions let's look at John: Lousy leader. Amazing servant.

He did not clutch his crown. He gave the Kingdom away. And Jesus called him the greatest of men.

Jesus: Now if anyone would be justified to gain a following for himself, it would be the one who alone is to be called "leader" – Christ. But just like John the Baptist, his followers deserted him in his time of greatest need. As he prayed in the garden his followers slept when he asked them to pray with him. Alone he walked the hill of Golgotha. Where were his followers? None but John (*there's that name again*) and some women were following him.

Jesus? By the world's definition: Lousy leader. Amazing servant.

He did not clutch his crown. He gave the Kingdom away.

While he was on this earth, he wasn't gaining for himself an earthly following. "My kingdom is not of this world," he said. It was about serving others. It was about stepping down into hell in order to lift others out of it. Servants step down into the slime. Into the filth. Into the fire. They step out of the light of glory in order to lift others out of the slime, out of the filth, out of the fire to set them in the light of glory.

Paul: He sits in a prison cell, execution imminent. Listen to these words to his brother Timothy: "Make every effort to come to me soon; for Demas, having loved this present world, has deserted me and gone to Thessalonica; Crescens has gone to

Galatia, Titus to Dalmatia. Only Luke is with me." (2 Timothy 4:9-11)

Turn around Paul. No one is following.

The Apostle Paul? Lousy leader. Amazing servant.

He did not clutch his crown. He gave the Kingdom away.

He rots in prison so others might be free.

Paul came under attack for his lousy leadership from the church in Corinth. When flashy men with eloquent speech came in and appealed to the human desire to have a king, they made themselves out to be these kings – "super" apostles. Here Paul fires back at the men that would be kings and the people who would stray from their devotion to Christ to follow such men:

> I wish that you would bear with me in a little foolishness; but indeed you are bearing with me. For I am jealous for you with a godly jealousy; for I betrothed you to one husband, that to Christ I might present you as a pure virgin. But I am afraid, lest as the serpent deceived Eve by his craftiness, your minds should be led astray from the simplicity and purity of devotion to Christ. . . Did I commit a sin in humbling myself

that you might be exalted, because I preached the gospel of God to you without charge? (2 Corinthians 11:1-3, 7)

Paul never stayed in one place long enough to gain a following for himself. He got down and lifted others up, set them on their feet, got them walking with Jesus and then he moved on.

His goal was that people would follow Jesus. His goal was that there would be a simple and pure devotion to Christ – not to himself, and not to "super" apostle kings.

Consider the amazing contrast between the Saul (King Saul) of the Old Testament and the Saul (Apostle Paul) of the New Testament.

King Saul	Apostle Paul (Formerly Saul)
• From peasantry to highest nobility	• From high nobility to imprisonment
• From poverty to privilege	• From privilege to poverty
• From weakness to warrior	• From warrior to weakness
• From serving God to fighting against God	• From fighting against God to serving God
• From humility to pride to humiliation	• From pride to humility to exaltation
• From servant to leader	• From leader to servant
• Dies clutching his crown	• Dies giving the Kingdom away

If we are seeking to gain a following, we are not only missing the point, we are missing the heart of the whole Gospel. We are not to be called "leaders." Jesus said this – not me. We are to be called servants.

Servants are always seeking to exalt others and not themselves. In the Kingdom this means we are always seeking to make others Jesus' followers and this means we are to direct them away from us and our personalities and direct them to Christ.

My prior concept of a "servant leader" was one that tells everyone what to do, gets a lot of followers for himself, and even though he is so great, so incredible, and so gifted in so many ways, he still shows up to banquets and serves tables and picks up dirty plates. "How amazing for such a gifted man to do such lowly tasks! Truly this guy is a servant leader."

Though it is fine

The mark of truly great leaders is not found in the vast army of people following them, but rather it is found in those few that they push up and beyond themselves - to do even greater things than they. These are the servant leaders that impact the lives of future generations for good.

to pick up dirty dishes, this is not what a biblical servant leader is. A servant leader is a Jonathan. He seeks not to build a kingdom and then to hold onto it at all costs. Instead he finds others upon whom the Holy Spirit rests and he hands it to them. He gives the Kingdom away.

A servant leader is a John the Baptist. "He – Jesus – must increase, and I must decrease." He gives the Kingdom away.

A servant leader is a Jesus. He steps into hell to lift others out of it. He gives up the crown, so that others will be crowned in righteousness. His kingdom is not of this world. He gives the Kingdom away.

A servant leader is a New Testament Saul (Paul). He points people to Christ and not himself. He pours his life into others not so they will follow him, but so that they will pour their lives into others as they follow Christ. He not only gives the Kingdom away, but he teaches others to do the same.

Leadership Style – A Matter
of Cultural Preference?

[Jesus'] ministry was clearly defined, and the alternatives to the illusion and temptations of the desert were spelled out. A choice was made – life abundant, full, and free for all. Make no mistake about it, the day that choice was made, Jesus became suspect. That day in the temple he sealed the fate already prepared for him. How was the world to understand one who rejected an offer of power and control?

Joan Campbell

Is it possible that we as Jesus' followers have this leadership thing all wrong? Upside down?

I was in a large church foyer the other day and there on the wall were pictures of all the many, many staff members. The pictures were arranged in a pyramid shape. Many pictures on the bottom, and one lone picture, larger than the rest, that had somehow – like the rich cream in milk – managed to find its way to the top, above all the rest.

All in the church seemed – at least from the picture – to work for him.

It reminded me of a picture I had just seen at a company that showed all the companies top managers and the CEO on top.

It reminded me a bit of *American Idol*, and how you can only have one winner.

It reminded me of a picture I'd seen of the President and his cabinet.

It reminded me a lot of my own culture.

Church leadership throughout history has often come to look just like the leadership in the culture that surrounds the church. The people of Israel cried out for a king. Why? The scriptures say it was because they wanted to be just like the other nations. They looked around them and felt left out. They wanted to be just like the rest. The church does the same thing today when it comes to leadership.

In parts of Africa where the chief rules, the church leadership rules in the same manner.

In Eastern Europe and Russia where the communists had ruled with an iron fist for so long, the church leaders do exactly the same.

In Asia, where there has been an emperor or king – there is authoritarian church leadership in every respect.

In the Latin America countries where one dictator ousts another, the Christian leaders often resemble them. Often they live in paranoia – desperately trying to keep power until someone muscles it from them.

In the U.S. we have the "CEO" style or the "celebrity" style. Or, if we are really lucky, we have a brilliant combination of these two qualities in one man who leads our church.

But no matter the style, every culture cries out for a king. And we who aspire to lead, the mere mortals that we are, gladly answer this cry.

The most gifted chief, the most ambitious party member, the most aggressive and eloquent dictator, the high power CEO or the most endearing celebrity – it is these men and women who rise to the top. And there they stay. And from there they call the shots, and those below listen and obey. Those who don't listen and obey – eventually leave and try to find a king they can better listen to and obey. And still others leave to find a place where they can rise to the top because the top place of honor has already been filled. And we know well how we so desire the place of honor. There is room only for one on top.

So this is the way it is. Always, at the core, it is the same: Someone on top of the ladder and the rest on varied rungs below him – the celebrity and his fans, the leader and his followers, the senior pastor and his junior flock, the king and his subjects. "That's just the way church leadership is in this part of the world." I have heard that this is a matter of local preference, a matter of culture. And indeed it is. But is this the way it should be?

Does Jesus say anything different? Does the Bible simply say we should be just like the world and adopt the leadership models we see around us?

Jesus stood everything on its head. Especially leadership. This pyramid, which exists in every culture, was turned upside down by Christ.

The Kingdom is like a mustard seed. Planted in the ground. A seed dead in the ground. And from it a sprout. A single shoot. Then a branch. Two, four, eight, sixteen. Soon too many to count, all with beautiful lush leaves until it has become a huge tree where the birds flock to simply rest in its branches.

A tree is an inverted pyramid. Jesus just turned the pyramid on its head.

Instead of being leaders on top, who by our gifts and talents and personalities are able to attract followers and then move them like pawns below us to fulfill the vision and goals we have, we are to be like Jesus who steps down and pushes everyone else up. The reason we have been given gifts is not so we can showcase them from up top, but so we can get down and use these gifts to push others up and far beyond us. Our place is at the bottom of the ladder pushing people to completeness in Christ. We are to be rejoicing in the cool freedom of the shade of the tree

> *We look forward to the time when the Power of Love will replace the Love of Power. Then will our world know the blessings of peace.*
> William Gladstone

that towers above us. But it means letting go of our crown, and giving the Kingdom away.

Jonathan – "You will be king, and I will be next to you."

John the Baptist – "He must increase, and I must decrease."

Jesus – "Truly, truly, I say to you, he who believes in Me, the works that I do shall he do also; and greater works than these shall he do; because I go to the Father." (John 14:12)

"But I tell you the truth, it is to your advantage that I go away; for if I do not go away, the Helper shall not come to you; but if I go, I will send Him to you." (John 16:7)

Paul – "Or did I commit a sin in humbling myself that you might be exalted, because I preached the gospel of God to you without charge?" (2 Corinthians 11:7)

The very nature of the Gospel insists that we climb down off our thrones of power and position and push others up into the fullness and likeness of Christ.

Do nothing from selfishness or empty conceit, but with humility of mind let each of you regard one another as more important than himself; do not merely look out for your own personal interests, but also for the interests of others. Have this attitude in yourselves which was also in Christ Jesus, who, although He existed in the form of God, did not regard equality with God a thing to be grasped, but emptied Himself, taking the form of a bond-servant, and being made in the likeness of men. And being found in appearance as a man, He humbled Himself by becoming obedient to the point of death, even death on a cross. (Philippians 2:3-9)

Clutching the crown is not a biblical option. How do we clutch this crown? Why do we? What does it mean to give the Kingdom away?

Who's Anointed Anyway?

Nearly all men can stand adversity, but if you want to test a man's character, give him power.
Abraham Lincoln

Saul had been anointed king. That anointing came from the prophet Samuel himself. Saul had received the Holy Spirit with power. God had chosen him to lead.

When David showed all the signs of having been anointed by God, Saul was self compelled to stop him. Saul's sin was a direct affront to God by trying to stop the one God had anointed. David, on the other hand, did not dare to raise his hand against Saul – the one God had also anointed as king.

Christian leaders. Pastors. Heads of organizations. CEO's. Heads of departments. Who is anointed anyway?

One of the pastors in the church where I serve was told by a key national Christian leader, "When you become senior pastor, you are God's anointed. The pulpit must be owned by the one whom God has anointed to lead."

My friend, upon receiving this advice, though he did not completely understand why, intuitively knew this advice to be wrong.

This Christian leader spoke of the pastor in terms that people speak of kings. "You are the anointed one." For a pastor to think of himself as a king of a certain domain is wrong and deadly.

> *"Pastor" is not a title, it is a gift. It is not something we are. It is a gift we have been given and are to utilize to serve others.*

And yet the people still cry out for a king. When they cry for a king, and when we as leaders harken unto that cry, King Saul will emerge and King Saul and all the people will suffer.

Here's the core message of the New Testament: Everyone who calls upon the name of Jesus is anointed. All those who are in Christ are royalty. We are all children of the King and anointed for service. The Apostle John makes this crystal clear: "But you have an anointing from the Holy One, and you all know." (1 John 2:20)

God has given everyone who calls on his name the power of the Holy Spirit and gifts that are given to be employed in loving and serving God and others. This is his anointing.

> And as for you, the anointing which you received from Him abides in you, and you have no need for anyone to teach you; but as His anointing teaches you about all things, and is true and is not a lie, and just as it has taught you, you abide in Him. (1 John 2:27)

"Pastor" is not a title, it is a gift. It is not something we are. It is a gift we have been given and are to utilize to serve others. If we think of ourselves as more anointed than those allotted to our charge – then we have missed the message of the Gospel.

There is another powerful reason people cry out for an earthly "king" to lead them in the spiritual realm. Laziness. Sloth. Quite simply, it is easier. It's easier and more efficient to have a man tell you what to do, than it is to seek God and his will for your life. To hear his voice is not easy. To obey it, even harder. The people of Israel begged God to speak through Moses instead of to them directly. It was too

> *It is easier to pay a pastor to feed me once a week than it is for me to open the Bible and then be diligent to study it.*

much for them to hear. It was also convenient for them in that they could blame Moses when things went wrong instead of seeing themselves to blame. In fact, Moses gets blamed for just about everything.

But God calls every follower of Jesus to personally seek his face. To individually and corporately seek his will. I admit – it is easier to pay a pastor to feed me once a week than it is for me to open the Bible and be diligent to study it. It is easier to have a man of God lead me in an eloquent prayer than it is to learn to pray. It is easier to let one man seek God on my behalf and on behalf of the Church and to let him tell me what he found out for my life than it is to seek God's will for my life and his will for me this very day. And it is definitely more fun to blame them and their lack of leadership when my life and my church turn sour. We simply prefer to pay our tax (tithe) and to hire another to do it for us. This attitude is flat out lazy and wrong. But it is even more wrong for me, as a leader, to cater to this sinful spiritual slothfulness, by exalting myself over the lazy as their king.

Do we as leaders believe we are the "true" anointed? If so, we may be the leaders Jesus refers to who "lord it over" others. A modern day equivalent for "lord it over" would be "seek to control."

Those who believe they are the "anointed" are like King Saul – they will overstep their boundary, and the people under them – who have the greatest potential – will be considered a threat. They'll be kept untrained, on a tight leash and ineffective.

Those leaders who see themselves as gifted for the purpose of equipping the anointed will seek to serve, build up, and unleash the entire body of Christ. The "anointed one" in the New Testament is every follower of Jesus – the whole body of Christ.

Those leaders who believe they are the anointed will believe and start to act as though they are the kings of the church or organization. When someone is doing something outside their control, they will seek to stop it and often crush the work of the Holy Spirit in others' lives – just like King Saul sought to do.

Ponder this question: Does anyone have the right to control the Holy Spirit? Or to think that they are the sole "anointed one" for the business at hand?

We as leaders so often, just like Saul, put a cap on the Kingdom. The Kingdom was meant to constantly overflow and yet we gifted leaders can use our gifts in such a way as to screw the cap on tight and to stop the overflowing of the Spirit in the body of Christ and in the Kingdom.

How so? "I am the best preacher – so I need to preach all the time." I have heard this said and have been arrogant enough to think such thoughts myself. First, who anointed me "best preacher?" Second, if I am good and really gifted, can I not raise up younger men even better than myself? This is the true challenge. This would model that this "kingdom" thing is not about what I can hold on to, but what I can give away.

If God has given me the responsibility to lead, and I use this authority to stay on top – to be "the man," to be the celebrity that draws all men to myself (convincing myself that it is really God people are being drawn to) – instead of using my gifts and talents to push many more up and beyond my abilities, then I have put a cap on the Kingdom. I have kept the Holy Spirit down. And I have set myself up. In fact, I have set myself up for ultimate failure.

There are two models here: I can use my gifts and talents to draw all men to rally around me and these God-given abilities of mine. Or I can use these gifts primarily to get down and to push others up so the Holy Spirit has freedom to use every man and woman in my congregation according to their gifts.

I've given these two models these two names:

One : *"Wow" them and they'll come*

Two: *Equip them and they'll go*

Here is how the two differ in a church setting:

"Wow" them and they'll come

A church has one primary teacher. He is such a good communicator that he is the speaker each week. People come to this church because he is so good and popular and he knows this is why they come. The days he leaves the church they must bring in another high powered celebrity communicator who people love just as much in order to keep people (and money) coming.

The music is professional and only the best five or six musicians play. In this environment, anyone else with musical gifts never gets the chance to get better and grow in the talents and abilities that God has given them.

People will come for the "wow" factor. In the West we live in a celebrity culture. Awesome talent is showcased for God's glory, but this begs the question - how then is the Kingdom given away? And how does that glorify God?

Equip them and they'll go

A church has a leader who is committed to raising up and training communicators. He is not the only preacher on Sunday, but often gives others who are gifted the opportunity to exercise and develop their gifts. He rejoices when he sees others grow to be better than himself. This is his goal so that when he is no longer around he will have given the Kingdom away to those more competent than himself. Many are now equipped to plant new churches. They are sent out. The Kingdom is stronger and bigger.

The music is led by people who raise up teams of musicians. These teams get better and better and many young musicians gain great competence in leading worship. Musicians and worship leaders are everywhere and are launched not only in this church but to strengthen churches everywhere. The Kingdom is advanced. It is given away.

If you want to grow *a* church – an instant little kingdom – my advice is that you go for option number one. "Wow" the people so their mouths drop open in amazement. Spare no cost and get the greatest speaker imaginable – preferably you. Get the greatest professional musicians money can buy. This really works!! In fact, I heard of a church plant recently that

> *"Wow" the masses with sheer talent. They will come. And a kingdom will grow as the masses look up to you – their celebrity king.*

was comprised of the nation's greatest songwriters – they had 3000 people the first week. 6000 the next. This model rocks. "Wow" the masses with sheer talent. They will come. And an instant kingdom will grow as the masses look up to you – their celebrity king.

If, however, you want to grow *the* Church – Christ's big Kingdom – get down and start pushing others up. Teach them to do the same. Every one with talents and gifts should push others ahead of themselves. Gifts, talents, and hearts will be strengthened and multiplied at first slowly but eventually at exponential rates. This is the Kingdom. It is not about being primarily concerned with getting people to come to a church service. It is about getting people to *go* – to their neighborhood, to their workplace, and even to the ends of the earth.

It is very much like Christ's parable of the Kingdom of God – it starts as a tiny mustard seed and grows into the largest of plants. It starts small. It starts with humility. It starts by taking the lowest seat and not the place of honor. A seed that dies and is laid in the ground. It starts by laying down our crown and giving the Kingdom away.

Once again consider the following scripture in light of the two scenarios above:

> Do nothing from selfishness or empty conceit, but with humility of mind let each of you regard one another as more important than himself; do not merely look out for your own personal interests, but also for the interests of others. Have this attitude in yourselves which was also in Christ Jesus, who, although He existed in the form of God, did not regard equality with God a thing to be grasped, but emptied Himself, taking the form of a bond-servant, and being made in the likeness of men. And being found in

appearance as a man, He humbled Himself by becoming obedient to the point of death, even death on a cross. Therefore also God highly exalted Him, and bestowed on Him the name which is above every name, that at the name of Jesus every knee should bow, of those who are in heaven, and on earth, and under the earth, and that every tongue should confess that Jesus Christ is Lord, to the glory of God the Father. (Philippians 2:3-11)

If anyone had the right to show off his crown and exercise his power it was Jesus. He existed in his very form as God. If anyone had the right to stand on top in glory and order and control those allotted his charge it was he. If there ever was a gifted individual that was capable of not only doing all things, but doing them right the first time, it was Jesus. But the perfect King gave all this up in order to serve those who were broken. He became weak to empower the powerless and to make capable the incapable. He gave up his rights and his position of power so that we might become all that we can be and reign with him for eternity. This is the message of the Bible, not some peripheral thought or biblical side point found on some rabbit trail. Jesus - the

King of the Universe - died a criminal's death in our place.   He did not clutch his crown.   He gave the Kingdom away.

Who then are we when we are determined to tighten our grip on the imaginary crowns of our self made kingdoms?

Command and Control or
Let the Holy Spirit Lead?

Often times a man's exceptional gifting takes him to a
level his character cannot sustain.
Ed Cole

Consider the two following views of leadership:

View 1: I have risen to the top for a good reason: God has given me special gifts – vision, eloquence and varied talents. It is my job to use this position of authority and influence to get each person below me to carry out the vision and purpose that God has given me. This is God ordained leadership.

View 2: I have risen to the top for good reason: God has given others special gifts – vision, eloquence, varied talents. It is my job to use this position of authority and influence, by getting down and to make sure each person below is empowered to carry out the vision and purpose God has given them. This is God ordained leadership.

Which is the right view? Is it just a matter of preference? Listen again to Jesus' words:

> And He said to them, "The kings of the Gentiles lord it over them... But not so with you, instead let him who is the greatest among you become as the least, and the leader as the servant. For who is greater, the one who reclines at the table, or the one who serves? Is it not the one who reclines at the table? But I am among you as the one who serves." (Luke 22:25-28)

Jesus clearly had a preference.

Listen to Paul:

> Now this expression, "He ascended," what does it mean except that He also had descended into the lower parts of the earth? He who descended is Himself also He who ascended far above all the heavens, that He might fill all things. And He gave some as apostles, and some as prophets,

and some as evangelists, and some as pastors and teachers, for the equipping of the saints for the work of service, to the building up of the body of Christ; until we all attain to the unity of the faith, and of the knowledge of the Son of God, to a mature man, to the measure of the stature which belongs to the fullness of Christ. (Ephesians 4:9-14)

Paul clearly had a preference.

Listen to Peter:

Therefore, I exhort the elders among you, as your fellow elder and witness of the sufferings of Christ, and a partaker also of the glory that is to be revealed, shepherd the flock of God among you, exercising oversight not under compulsion, but voluntarily, according to the will of God; and not for sordid gain, but with eagerness; nor yet as lording it over those allotted to your charge, but proving to be examples to the flock. And when the Chief Shepherd appears, you will receive the unfading crown of glory. You younger men, likewise, be subject to your elders; and all of you, clothe yourselves with humility toward one another, for God is opposed to the proud, but gives grace to the humble. Humble yourselves, therefore, under the mighty hand of God, that He may exalt you at the proper time. (1 Peter 5:1-6)

Peter clearly had a preference.

Leadership style is not a matter of preference or of culture. Biblical leaders need to get out of their high place, humble themselves and build others up. And they should teach others to do the same. Instead of an organization where we all are trying to climb by stepping on top of others and seeking to impose our vision and gifts upon everyone else, we can have a place where everyone is seeking to build everyone else up.

> **Biblical leaders need to get out of their high place, humble themselves and build others up. And they should teach others to do the same.**

If the "senior" pastor shows up on Sundays and he is always front and center, what has just been modeled?

When the "senior" pastor shows up Sunday morning and sits in the back while a man 15 years younger is given a chance to teach the Word, what has just been modeled?

When the head of a Christian organization shows up to the meeting to make sure all are in line with his goals and vision for the next year, what has just been modeled?

When the head of a Christian organization gets together individually with each under his charge to hear and listen to dreams and vision these people have for the organization and their own lives for the coming year, gleans from these meetings, and then he shows up to a meeting to align his team, what has just been modeled?

Who is the visionary?

The body of Christ has one head. And that is Christ. Listen to the scriptures:

> And He put all things in subjection under His feet, and gave Him as head over all things to the church, which is His body, the fullness of Him who fills all in all." (Ephesians 1:22-23)

We are to grow up in all aspects into Him, who is the head, even Christ, from whom the whole body, being fitted and held together by that which every joint supplies, according to the proper working of each individual part, causes the growth of the body for the building up of itself in love. (Ephesians 4:15-16)

Let no one keep defrauding you of your prize by delighting in self-abasement and the worship of the angels, taking his stand on visions he has seen, inflated without cause by his fleshly mind, and not holding fast to the head, from whom the entire body, being supplied and held together by the joints and ligaments, grows with a growth which is from God. (Colossians 2:18-19)

We clearly see there is one head – Jesus. Jesus dwells in and fills his church – every single member – not just one man who tells us the way it should be. The body builds itself up in love. It is not the job of one, or even a select few. It is the job of the whole body.

I heard a tragic statement recently that is all too true about the church. A mission pastor said, "If the senior pastor is not behind missions 100 percent and if it's not his vision then missions just won't happen like it should in your church." His solution to this problem was "Try your best to convert your senior pastor to missions."

My solution was a bit different. I wanted to find this senior pastor and chew him out (the human side of me coming out). Who did he think he was carrying the sole vision for the church? I was hired by my church, because Stu, the lead pastor, saw missions

> *The body builds itself up in love. It is not the job of one, or even a select few. It is the job of the whole body.*

in the Bible but did not have the vision for it, but I did. He hired me and set me loose to empower others and set them loose. Senior pastors should find those who eat and live missions, and then get behind them to empower them to bring missions to the body. There are hundreds of passionate visionaries in our churches – and it is a leader's job to make sure they are discipled, tapped into, and unleashed. God's heart is big, and it's arrogant for me as a leader to think my dream and vision encompasses all God has.

God wants leaders who find those who have a bigger heart for the many various elements of God's dream and then empower them to make the dream come true. That is humility. That is a servant. That is a New Testament leader.

So who is anointed? The leader or the people? There is a doctrine about that called the priesthood of all believers. All. All believers are anointed. Not just the leader. "But you are a chosen race, a royal priesthood, a holy nation, a people for God's own possession, that you may proclaim the excellencies of Him who has called you out of darkness into His marvelous light." (1 Peter 2:9)

What should be the goal of the pastor? To feed the sheep or to take them where they can feed themselves? Shepherds in biblical times led their sheep to pastures and let them feed themselves. They did not bottle and grain feed them like they do today in the developed world. The adage, "You can give a man a fish and feed him for a day, or teach him to fish and feed him for a lifetime" applies to church leaders as well. To send out the message in our preaching that "you – the sheep – can't possibly understand the scriptures without getting my constant Greek commentary and brilliant insights on them" is the wrong message to send. A "you can understand this book – so get into it" message is the right one. The Holy Spirit has anointed them to understand.

We as leaders are not supposed to draw all men to ourselves – so the masses come to us for nourishment, direction, and vision. We are to raise and build up self-feeders who discern the Holy Spirit's direction and vision for their lives and ministries. I have heard of pastors telling those in the congregation whom to marry and whom to date – controlling even the small details of their lives. This is not their job. They are to teach people how to make these biblically principled decisions and how to walk in the power of the Holy Spirit. Leaders are never told to be the Holy Spirit.

Recently a young couple, Peter and Jenn, whom I had poured a chunk of my life into, came in to talk about where God was leading them in missions. I naturally wanted them to go where I had been – to work with Muslims in Central Asia. But they believed God was leading them to work in Australia. At first I was a bit sad, but I asked how they had come to this conclusion. I found God had led them in so many specific ways. Over the past few years I had spent hours with Peter talking about all kinds of things including how to discern God's leading in our lives. And here he was living it. What a cool story of God's leading. But Australia? Expensive! I, as their overseer, would never have recommended such a place. To raise that much support would have been my worst personal nightmare.

A businessman in our church came to me furious that my team and I had given the green light for them to go to such an expensive place. His view of leadership was that I should decide where to send people and then send people there. Plug and Play. Command and control. "You just can't send people wherever they want to go," he said.

It was so clear to me that Jesus was leading Peter and Jenn to Australia. It was not about me leading them anywhere – but leading them to Christ – and then letting him lead them. In just a week they will be leaving for training and then Australia, and I could not be happier.

When Paul talked about the church gathering in 1 Corinthians 12-14 he was most concerned that people get to use their gifts. He did not say, "Let the one who is the leader figure out what God wants, and then let him plug people into these roles."

Here is what he did say:

> But one and the same Spirit works all these things, distributing to each one individually just as He wills. (1 Corinthians 12:11)

> What is the outcome then, brethren? When you assemble, each one has a psalm, has a teaching, has a revelation, has a tongue, has an interpretation. Let all things be done for edification. (1 Corinthians 14:26)

The Church is not, and the Kingdom is not a one man show.

The church for too long has been about empowering the one with the pastor/teacher gifts to be all he can be at the expense of the church members. "Are you a businessman? Then make money so you can give it to empower the leaders with the gifts to do the work of the ministry. You - the people - need to give so we - the anointed - can do ministry." We leaders are often guilty of using other's gifts and resources to elevate ourselves, our position, and our ego to new heights. This is tragically and sinfully upside down.

Jesus calls us leaders to be getting down and lowering ourselves in order to lift others up. Not commanding and controlling our people to meet our own goals and objectives. We are to trust, as we build into them and teach them to be self feeders, for the Holy Spirit to begin to direct and use them mightily in ministry. Everyone in the body of Christ is called to minister and it is job of the leaders to make sure all are empowered to be the best ministers they can be. This is the leader's calling – to serve others. When the businessman, when the mechanic, when the housewife, when everyone in the body is equipped and empowered to do the ministry God has gifted them to do, the Kingdom of God will grow in astounding ways. It may not look at all like we had originally envisioned – but that is the Body of Christ. It is his body and it is his vision that counts. We are not the head – Christ alone is. And through his Holy Spirit he will lead his people.

Why Discipleship So Often Fails

The love of liberty is the love of others; the love of power is the love of ourselves.
William Hazlitt

Discipleship. Making disciples. It is the thrust of the Great Commission. But do most churches do it well? Do most churches do it at all? Are the older men out there with younger men pouring into each other's lives helping the other to do the things Jesus taught us? Are the older women passing the baton to the younger helping them guide their kids through the teenage years and coming alongside young moms to give guidance and strength?

Most churches wish this was going on everywhere. Most leaders when asked about how their climate of discipleship is in their church admit to this being a major point of weakness.

Why is it so weak? There is a huge reason for this. It simply is not modeled by the leaders. King Saul had no disciples. They were a threat to him. He tried to spear them to the wall. How often do you read of Saul's mighty men? You don't. He was out trying to kill them.

Jonathan, however, modeled what it meant to disciple. He handed the Kingdom away to David. David as a leader had men who surpassed even him in his exploits, and they got the credit for it. You read all about David's mighty men. Jonathan modeled discipleship and David carried it on.

When we as leaders have the high need to be the kingpin, the one on top, the one seen, the one heard, the one in charge, then we are not discipling people. As long as we are always front and center, we will never model discipleship for our people to see. But when we, as skilled preachers, launch young men and fine tune them, and when people come to us and say – "Hey, he is better than you!" – then Christ-like discipleship has been modeled. Our people will see it and begin to get it. And they just might start doing it.

My uncle earned his black belt in karate while going to veterinary school. His "master" was amazing at martial arts and an amazing instructor. One day after an intense workout he called my uncle over to himself. "Bill, you are getting good. But you will never be as good as me."

My uncle was a bit taken aback from the remark and inquired, "Why can't I be as good as you?"

His master's reply shocked him. "Because there are things that I know that I will never teach you. No, you will never become as good as me."

If all teachers had the need to be the greatest – like this karate master did – it would spell the eventual demise of the sport of karate. Imagine my Uncle Bill becoming really good but not as good as his master, and adopting the same attitude toward his students: not allowing them to surpass him. Each generation of karate would get worse and worse and soon a black belt could be achieved with a wild kick in the air.

The Kingdom of God is like a mustard seed. It goes down and into the ground and every generation gets higher and higher and soon it is a high tree where all the birds nest in the branches.

When I stay on top and do not release others to surpass me – I am not about growing the Kingdom – but I am saying that it stops right here with me. I am as good as it gets.

That is the King Saul Syndrome at its worst. And we see its symptoms everywhere.

Bob, a fellow pastor and friend who serves on the team with me here at our church, told me a story of meeting with a friend of his who was now pastoring a large church. Bob asked him, "So who else preaches at your church?"

"Just me," came his reply.

"You have a church of several thousand and you are the sole preacher?"

"Well, yes," the pastor replied matter-of-factly.

"You mean to tell me that there is no one else in the body who is gifted to teach?"

His silence spoke volumes.

"So who preaches when you are on vacation?" Bob inquired.

"I get someone to come in from outside."

Bob did not have to ask why. He knew. To allow someone gifted from within to preach would mean that there would be those in the church who would start asking to have him preach again and again. It was a threat to the king. Bob asked a few more questions to show this man his King Saulish ways. For the first time he saw what he was doing.

This little story is by no means an exception. I asked the sister of the celebrity pastor of one of the nation's largest churches this question: "Which of the 20+ pastors on the church staff gets to preach when your brother is out of town?"

> *How will this pastor's people ever learn anything of discipleship when he doesn't trust one of his own to take his place even for one Sunday?*

"None of them. He always gets someone from outside to come in and preach."

I could not believe it. 20+ pastors. 15,000 people. Not one he would trust with his kingdom. He just couldn't give it away. How will his people ever learn anything of discipleship when he doesn't trust one of his own to take his place even for a single Sunday?

I heard a story of a senior pastor who was a great theologian. He had a huge church. Someone told me that every single worship song – whether it be in the service, in the youth groups, in the women's ministry, or in the children's ministry – must first be approved by him, the senior pastor.

I understand the desire to be doctrinally sound. There are a lot of songs that are worthless and others that teach bad theology. But what I can't understand is this: In a church 10,000 strong, is there not one other decent theologian? Has this pastor discipled no one? Each department could easily have someone trained enough and given authority to make theological decisions regarding their songs. God has given every believer authority. Could this pastor give it to no one?

In a church like this discipleship is not modeled. Control is. There is a cap screwed tightly on to the top of this kingdom. We leaders must be building up and empowering and unleashing. We can delude ourselves by thinking that because I am not jealous of a younger man, then I am not like King Saul. Truth is we might be even worse than King Saul in this one way: We kill future leaders by simply never giving them a chance. We abort them before they are even born. Even Saul gave David the chance to fight Goliath.

Remember Jonathan, John the Baptist, Jesus and Paul. They gave the Kingdom away. Paul, like Jonathan, poured his life into a younger man, Timothy. And listen to what Paul (the converted Saul) gave as a charge to Timothy at the end of his life: "These things that I have entrusted you in the presence of many witnesses, teach to faithful men, who will in turn teach others." (2 Timothy 2:2)

Making disciples is about giving the Kingdom away. If we as leaders do not model this in our church in our most visible role, then can we really expect others to do it? Is it really any wonder why so little real discipleship is taking place?

Church plants in America are so often about the show – the right music, the right publicity, the right man to speak. They want the church service to be awesome. Paul started churches by discipling people.

We need to step down, take off our crowns, and disciple others by giving the Kingdom away.

The Pain of Letting Go

Power does not corrupt. Fear corrupts... perhaps the fear of a loss of power.
John Steinbeck

Why does the King Saul Syndrome grab hold of so many Christian leaders? Maybe I should rephrase that question. Why does it grab a hold of all of us? Why does giving the Kingdom away come with such difficulty? Why does it threaten us to have others surpass us in their abilities?

> *Why does it threaten us to have others surpass us in their abilities?*

I asked this question to the country directors of one of the world's largest relief agencies. They all confessed their struggle with wanting to hold on, and agreed that it was this King Saul Syndrome that was keeping the work of God from moving forward in their countries.

The answers they gave cut right to the heart – exposing us for who we are in our frail humanity. Why is it so hard to give the Kingdom away? Why would we not want others to surpass us for the sake of the Kingdom? Here was their list in the order they shouted them out:

- Selfishness
- Pride
- Self worth
- Appearance
- Stature
- Money
- Fame
- Protection/preservation/security
- Fear
- Unfinished business
- Being a law unto yourself
- Desire to stay on top
- The intoxication that power brings
- Ego feeding
- Self image

- Reputation
- Making and keeping a name for yourself
- Affirmation/acceptance from others
- Identity
- A core belief that "I really am the best"
- The belief that "I am indispensible"
- A lack of understanding God's truth

These answers were given in no time at all. All the leaders knew exactly why it was so hard to give the Kingdom away. When Jonathan handed it away to David, it was no easier. He likely had to deal with most of these issues. But still he made the choice. John the Baptist. Jesus. The Apostle Paul. All said "no" to the position of power, and instead put the Kingdom first. That "no" to self never came easy. The "yes" to the Kingdom always comes with a price. But with the right decision comes freedom, and the Kingdom grows.

Let's discuss a few of these reasons in more detail.

Pride.

Power is intoxicating. It feeds our pride. To be king. To be on top. To stay on top.

Pride. Let's face it. It is in all of us. It was the universe's first and original sin and it was found in the most gifted and glorious angel. And Lucifer was cast down from heaven to earth as a result.

In Tolkien's classic "The Lord of the Rings" there are nine kings who were all given rings of power. At first, all used the rings to do good, but this power became intoxicating and soon all they wanted was more. The need to retain this power became controlling. They became the living dead. King Saul was just like them.

> *Let's face it. It is in all of us. It was the universe's first and original sin.*

We in our frail humanity will become just like them – just like Saul. I am a master at convincing myself that it is for the Kingdom, while all the time it really is for my own little kingdom. This allure to power is in me. It is me. But it is not Jesus.

Jonathan knew the answer. The solution was showed to us in Jesus. The only cure for the intoxication of power and addiction to power is to give it away. This may be the hardest thing we have ever done, but when we do, there comes a freedom that surpasses all human reason. We are no longer like the living dead Tolkien describes – but we are truly alive. We are free from the love of power – for a little while anyway.

After my first trip to Africa, and upon seeing the great needs on the continent, I came back changed. I wanted everyone else in my congregation to be changed as well. Now God has gifted me in communicating through stories, and he has given me gifts of creativity. The stories helped people get it. But I wanted to do more. I wanted to change hearts everywhere. And there was no greater medium to affect hearts than through video.

I, in my mind, dreamed and planned what this video would be, and I envisioned how it could change hearts. I was excited to get back to Africa to shoot this video.

I had one problem: I did not have the skills to shoot the video. I had the vision, I had the dream, but I didn't have the skill.

"Seth!" I thought. He had shot film for the Discovery Channel. I had seen some of his work. He'd probably love to go to Africa. With Seth's help, my dream could come true. I called Seth. He was excited and said yes. My imagination and the creative side of me went wild. I really believed this video could not only help change the hearts of my own congregation but it could be used by churches all over the U.S. for kingdom purposes. Seth and I set a date to get together to plan.

I had come up with right title of the video, had planned the different shots and the script was coming together in my head. The day finally arrived for the two of us to get together so I could share my dream with the one who could help make it a reality. I was excited.

I shook hands with Seth as he got out of his car. And I will not forget his first statement.

"I am so excited," he said. "I have a great idea for the video!"

All my excitement died with that statement but I dared not show it on my face. Wait. I was the one with the great idea. I had invited him to help make my great idea become a reality. He was not supposed to have a great idea. I was the visionary here. What was I supposed to say? I couldn't very well say, "I don't want to hear it!" But that is exactly what I was thinking. Perhaps I could have said, "Well, let me tell you mine first." But that seemed a bit rude.

So being trapped, I said, "Let me hear your idea."

And he began. "I want it to be called, 'The Journey is the Destination,' and I want to start shooting it here and..." As he went on with great clarity of his own vision, I started thinking, "*Who is this guy? He hasn't even been to Africa. Doesn't he know that I'm the boss? I asked him to help me.*" Meanwhile, as he went on and on, I smiled and pretended to listen.

Finally he finished and said, "But it's fine if we don't do it this way. Now what are your ideas?"

I did not know I had enlisted a guy with his own dreams and ideas. I wanted someone to help me fulfill mine – which I believed to be God-endorsed. What was I to do? His idea was good, but I honestly believed mine to be better. Much better. And my heart was set. But I was torn for I had just told the story of Jonathan at a church retreat. Jonathan gave the Kingdom away.

I wanted to become a salesman and convince him of the superiority of my plan. I wanted to tell him that once he gets to Africa he'll see why what I had planned was so critical for people to see. I wanted...

I opened my mouth and the words that came out shocked me. "Seth, we are going to do it. Yours is a great idea. Let's do it."

That was not what my heart and mind were screaming. But that is what came out.

Seth sort of just stood there dumbfounded.

"Are you serious?" he inquired.

Now was my chance to recant.

"Yep, I am serious. Let's make your film happen."

"Are you sure?" he asked incredulously.

"I'm sure." My dream had just died and with it a part of me.

"It is just that in all my years in working with the church, no one has ever said that to me."

No one had ever let him loose. His shock turned to an expression of excitement and even great joy. My dream had died, but his dream had just come alive.

And then came freedom. What joy overflowed in my own heart. I had given the Kingdom away. The thought of it had been so painful, but once done I felt nothing but freedom and joy.

Seth today lives in Africa. He is serving agency after agency in the poorest and most dangerous of places. He serves the local church there as well in amazing ways – empowering them to do what they never thought possible. He actually is one of the most amazing missionaries I know. It frightens me to think, "What if I had clutched my crown and made Seth do what I wanted." I came so close. But instead, Seth is now one who models giving the Kingdom away. He has taught me so much.

> *I had given the Kingdom away. The thought of it had been so painful. But once done, I felt nothing but freedom and joy.*

Money. Protection. Preservation.

Many people in ministry get their job because they, of all the applicants, did the best song and dance when candidating for the pastoral position. They performed the best and therefore they were hired. When someone else comes along that sings and dances better, it is not only a threat to their pride and ego, it is a threat to their livelihood. If I was hired because they like my preaching best, and I let this young guy preach and they like him better – then what will keep the people from wanting to hire him and place him above me?

King Saul takes over and the young David is kept down and kept out.

Paul reminds Timothy that the Kingdom is to be first. We are never to be in ministry for the financial security it provides. The early church was not as professionally led as it is today. When our own livelihood is threatened by the gifted in our own body or organization, there is a very human threat. We must always remember to be "building the Kingdom" and not "using the church" to give us worldly security. God is our provider.

Many pastoral search committees are really unbiblical in their standard for whom they hire. It is more like an American Idol contest than it is looking for a man of God who desires to build disciples who surpass him. I would dare to say that most search committees – which we don't see in the Bible because leadership was raised from within – will decide on a candidate by who is the best preacher. Who will make the best "king" or figure head? Whose teaching will draw the most followers? The question should be: Who will raise and train up the most servant leaders for the Kingdom?

The number of hours put into a sermon each week just so he can keep his job, often takes the man of God out of what his job really is – to equip the saints for the work of service.

Look at the New Testament – I dare you – and try to find the sermon and its deliverer as the main attraction to a church. But today, celebrity worship has pervaded our culture and has poisoned the Church. The people want a king – but we as servant leaders must remind them there is no king but Jesus, and that they are the anointed ministers.

A great friend and fellow pastor, Bob, has been mentoring a pastor named Andre in Russia. Bob challenged this pastor to raise up other men to preach so he would not be the only one. What a foreign concept this was. At first this idea seemed a bit threatening. But seeing that it was biblical, he began. This month there will be a church retreat where other men in his church will be doing all the teaching and preaching. Andre is so excited. He now sees the freedom and joy that comes in giving the Kingdom away. Will they be better than Andre? Will Andre lose his job as a result? Maybe. But he just does not care. He has become like Jonathan and like Jesus. Dosvidaniya King Saul.

My very own church was started by very young men. Now 33 years later these same men are not so young. Will the church die with the leaders? We are faced with the reality that if we hang on to "job security" it will simply kill the Kingdom. We have got to give it away, and it brings the greatest joy simply to be trying.

A core belief that "I am the best"

I've heard of a pastor who told his leadership team very close to these words: "I am the best preacher – so I will preach and teach all of the time. These guys are the best musicians, so they will lead worship all of the time." It was true. He is the best in the church. And so were those musicians. But he might as well have just said, "We have our kingdom and its rulers."

> *As arrogant as this may sound, it might really be true. You might really be the best at what you do.*

How then will gifts be developed? What if someone in his congregation has even a greater gift to preach than his own but it has simply not been developed. He has said in no uncertain terms, "That man's gifts will not be developed here under my leadership."

I, personally, don't want to stand before the Lord having made that declaration.

Just because you are presently "the best" does not mean you should not develop others by giving them opportunities to grow. Actually, being the best likely means that you are the most equipped of God to develop others. And if you do not use it to develop others, to push them up to surpass even you, then you are missing the heart of Jesus who desired that his disciples surpass even him when it came to the great things he did.

In Ephesians 4 Paul says that God has made some to be apostles, some evangelists, some teachers. To do what? To apostle-ize, evangelize, teach? Sure, they did these things, but the primary job is *"to equip the saints to do the work of the ministry."* Are you a gifted teacher? Equip and train the saints to teach others who will in turn teach others. Are you an evangelist? Don't do all the evangelism, but use your gift to help others become better in reaching their friends for Christ who then will help those friends reach others. The Kingdom of God has no cap. No end. But when we build a ministry around us and our gifts – our little kingdom has a big cap on it.

I like to think of myself as the best story teller at our church (which I am sure is not true –but please don't tell me that). I especially enjoy doing dramatic monologues where I take on the character of someone in the Bible. I had always just simply done these. I liked to. I was gifted at it. Others liked me for it. And never had I thought about teaching others to do it, or giving others a chance.

> *The Kingdom of God has no cap. No end. But when we build a ministry around ourselves and our gifts – our little kingdom has a big cap on it.*

Actually, I had taught others in Africa to do this, but there they were no threat to the identity I had achieved for myself at my home church.

Well, recently I was scheduled to be the Centurion who was at the cross and tomb of Christ. They were counting on me. But I had double booked. I had to be elsewhere for two of the scheduled times. I did the unthinkable. I asked someone else to do it for me. He came and watched me the first time, then did it the next two times.

He did an amazing job. I like to think I did better, but who am I fooling? Why had I never thought of this before? Well, because I was the best! Or so I chose to believe. How lame of me.

I just recently made a decision to train others to do this. If I train a small army of storytellers, then children's ministry at our church will have plenty of storytellers and others will be equipped. I can be 100 times more effective. But I have to realize there is a cost. With the advancement of the Kingdom, there will come some storytellers that get better than me. I might no longer be the best. It is funny how my perspective has changed since understanding the heart of Jonathan, for I don't think I will find myself shedding any tears.

The belief that "I am indispensible."

Some of us leaders delude ourselves into believing that the Kingdom just couldn't make it without us. "If I were to stop preaching every

Sunday, this church would just die." Yes, the church you built around yourself and your personality might just die. But the Kingdom of God will almost surely be better because of it. If your church dies because you are not there – what kind of church was it? Were they following Jesus or you?

I have heard it said that Martin Lloyd Jones, perhaps the greatest preacher of the last century, greatly lamented the fact that Westminster Chapel's attendance dropped dramatically once he retired. "I have not built a church, I have built myself a preaching station."

I am afraid that many other preachers upon their retirement and subsequent decline and meltdown of their church, might find a smug sense of satisfaction. "Wow. Look how much I was needed."

I heard of one leader of a very large church who acknowledged, "I have to spend twenty to thirty hours a week on sermon prep because I know the reality is that they come to hear me."

Is that the kind of ministry we are asked to build? One that orbits around our personality and gifts? Would anyone stop following Christ because this guy stepped off the high rung and gave other gifted men in his 10,000 member congregation the chance to exercise their preaching and teaching gifts? Not only would these young men grow in their ability to preach, they would see "giving the Kingdom away" modeled by their leader. But as it is they are not given a chance, and they are not seeing it modeled. When they leave this church to start their own (only way to have a chance) – you can almost bet they will seek to build a ministry that orbits around themselves. After all it draws 10,000 people.

> *Is that the kind of ministry I am asked to build? One that revolves and orbits around my personality and my gifts?*

This pastor, by allowing other gifted men to preach, could then clearly see how many in his flock are followers of Jesus and who is following merely after him and his brilliant teaching.

As this church grows the pastor can make a choice. "Will I train up other communicators for other churches, or will I just video tape myself and play that at the other church campuses?"

The Bible says we are to make disciples who will teach others who will in turn teach others. That takes work. But a video of a celebrity will be more effective – at least for today, and for this little kingdom of the moment.

Just because the people cry out for a celebrity king doesn't mean we are meant to be that king. In fact, we are constantly being called to give the Kingdom away.

If we are building **"a"** church or **"a"** movement that is dependent upon us and our talents and great abilities, we are building a house of cards. A kingdom for a moment. A kingdom that will come crashing down.

But **"the"** Church is not like this. We must realize that God can and might choose to dispense of us at any moment. All those we have poured into, trained, and pushed up and beyond us and our own talents will continue on, and will in turn build more. Such a movement starts with realizing that: "We are nothing. His Kingdom is everything." It starts with the prayer, "Thy kingdom come." Not, "My kingdom come." We must learn to let go of the crown. The Kingdom is to be given away.

Identity. Affirmation. Name.

Often our position and title become our identity. To let go of my title, "pastor" or "president" or "bishop," is to let go of who I am at the core. I know a dear pastor and friend who answered the phone from his own home, "Pastor Dan. Can I help you?" His name was "Pastor Dan." When it became very clear that it was time for him to move out of this position and into another, he could not do it. It had become his identity. The whole church was split and at the core, I believe, it was because his identity was in his position rather than in Christ.

Imagine the young Jonathan always being told that he was the heir to the throne and that one day he would be king, which I am sure his father taught him. Yet Jonathan never allowed that to become who he was. When the test came – he passed.

I love preaching. I love to study the Word. I love to meditate on it. I love taking on our culture and its wild ways by wielding the sword of the Spirit. I love being creative. I love impacting lives for good.

I also love the attention I get. I love the compliments. I love having people laugh at my jokes. Now I am learning to love something even more – giving others a chance to do what I love.

A couple of years ago I was hit between the eyes with the realities of preaching. It was at a time that I wanted to preach more and more – and then an e-mail woke me up to the realities of life.

I received a letter from the secretary of the pastor I grew up under. I probably listened to 300 sermons from this man. Steve was a good preacher and faithful to the word. Here is what the e-mail said: "We are going to have a party for Steve celebrating his 30th year of ministry. Please write us and tell us what Steve's preaching has meant to you throughout the years."

Steve's preaching? Why not Steve? Why not "Tell us what Steve has meant to you throughout the years"? I actually think I know why. He firmly believed in his call to preach the Word. That was his calling. That is what he did every weekend except while on vacation.

I will answer the question. What did his preaching mean to me? Chalk it up to attention deficit disorder – but I could not remember a thing. Not one sermon. Not one point. I did remember one illustration because he mentioned Playboy magazine (very impressionable 6th grade ears) from up front – but I was not proud of remembering that alone and did not wish to mention that to his secretary. So, I'd heard some 300 sermons and I could write nothing.

But if she had asked about Steve and what he meant to me, that would have been different. When I was in seminary, I was a youth intern at the church and got to meet with Steve one on one, once a week. I remember almost everything we talked about in those meetings. He was so personal. We became friends. An older man to the younger. He was about 15 years older than me. Just like Jonathan was to David. The things he shared with me about ministry, marriage, family and living changed the course of my life. I think I am married to the amazing woman who is my wife because of the wise advice he gave. He gave me insights as I prepared to get married and helped me understand the nature of raising kids.

Today, I still quote him all the time from those meetings I had with him one on one. He even let me preach, and I knew that was huge for him. That showed me I had abilities and a passion in that arena. As a friend and mentor he directed the course of my life. What an amazing friend!

But that was not what the letter asked. "What did Steve's preaching mean to you?" Again I racked my brains. I remembered when he came to a high school Bible study and spoke. I hid at the top of the stairs (I was only twelve and not in high school yet) and he talked about dating to the small group. I remember that talk to this very day. Individually, and in the small groups I remembered Steve's words of wisdom. But the question was about his preaching. I had no answer.

So here I am at a big church and I love to preach, but I am so humbled that 30 years from now no one will remember what I have said in front of the masses. But, if I am a Jonathan to others. If I pour my life into them. If I get small and down with them and take a step below them. If I give others opportunities to grow. If I constantly am pushing others up. If I let those younger than I do greater

works than my own. If I give the Kingdom away –
these things will be remembered and will impact
future generations and future movements. Most
importantly: Jesus will be pleased and his name
honored.

So why do I want to be "big," "up front" and "on
top?"

The Kingdom does not come from on top.
Remember the mustard seed. Remember the grain of
wheat. It starts in the ground.

> Truly, truly, I say to you, unless a grain of wheat
> falls into the earth and dies, it remains by itself
> alone; but if it dies, it bears much fruit. He who
> loves his life loses it; and he who hates his life in
> this world shall keep it to life eternal. If anyone
> serves Me, let him follow Me; and where I am,
> there shall My servant also be; if anyone serves
> Me, the Father will honor him. (John 12:24-26)

We've looked at a large list of reasons on why it
is so hard to give the Kingdom away. To do it, we
must die. We must die to each one of them –
*selfishness, pride, self worth, appearance, stature,
money, fame, protection/preservation/security, fear,
unfinished business, being a law unto ourselves, desire*

to stay on top, the intoxication that power brings, ego feeding, self image, reputation, name for ourselves, affirmation and acceptance from others, identity, core belief that "I really am the best," the belief that "I am indispensible," and a lack of understanding.

When our fingers are finally pried, one by one, from the crown we so want to believe is ours; when the King Saul in us dies and our own personal kingdoms die with him, from that lone

The Kingdom does not come from on top. Remember the mustard seed. Remember the grain of wheat. It starts in the ground.

seed in the ground the Kingdom will grow. And we will find the joy and freedom that Jonathan found in giving it all away.

What if My Leader is a King Saul?

For the LORD delivered you (Saul) into my hand today, but I (David) refused to stretch out my hand against the Lord's anointed. Now behold, as your life was highly valued in my sight this day, so may my life be highly valued in the sight of the LORD, and may He deliver me from all distress.

1 Samuel 26:23-24

This short book has given ample biblical ammunition if one should choose to lead an attack on a leader who is clearly trapped in the grip of the King Saul Syndrome. But to do so would be unbiblical, unwise, and unloving. In other words – wrong. If ever someone had the right and opportunity to attack a King Saul leader, it was David. Twice. Yet his words were the same each time: *"Who can stretch out his hand against the Lord's anointed and be without guilt?"*

David would not attack him. He had a high view of authority for it was God given.

So what are we to do?

If God calls Christian leaders to build the Kingdom by serving and empowering others and by letting those who are better than they are to exercise those gifts, but the "Christian" leader over us is primarily concerned with controlling his own personal kingdom by keeping those gifted down – what are we to do?

First, we must realize that we are all King Saul to some degree. If we have a desire to attack our leader with the examples in this book – this probably shows that King Saul is alive and well and kicking inside of us. It may well be your own selfish ambition that angers you. As Jesus says, "First, get rid of the log in your own eye."

> What is the source of quarrels and conflicts among you? Is not the source your pleasures that wage war in your members? You lust and do not have; so you commit murder. And you are envious and cannot obtain; so you fight and quarrel. (James 4:1-2)

Love gives the opportunity to change. That is what David did. He confronted Saul in his irrational jealousy, and so did Jonathan. Perhaps this book may be used to expose the King Saul tendencies in us all. Lovingly and prayerfully look for an opportunity to challenge and share these principles with your leader. Loving confrontation, well planned and executed may be what that person needs and what God wants.

Here is a hard question: *When is it time to leave?*

I am committed to the principles of leading in a Jonathan-like manner. I will teach these principles to all those I am training and discipling. If I have a "King Saul" leader above me, he may quickly become upset, just as Saul did with Jonathan. I have seen this happen to a great friend.

So if you are in this situation, pray that the leader above you will be influenced by your training and teaching. But realize this: he may ask you to stop teaching it or even to leave and go elsewhere, for servant leadership may be inadvertently exposing the kind of leader he is and is not. If he asks you to leave, rejoice and do not leave angrily or with a bitter heart.

Once you leave, do not lob grenades back into the camp that you have just left.

David had to leave – but he always respected Saul. He left Saul in God's hand:

> As the LORD lives, surely the LORD will strike him, or his day will come that he dies, or he will go down into battle and perish. The LORD forbid that I should stretch out my hand against the Lord's anointed; but now please take the spear that is at his head and the jug of water, and let us go. (1 Samuel 26:10-11)

It is not your job to take your leader down or to get him out. God can do that just fine without you. David realized this and so should you. God puts spreading strife among brothers among those things which He hates. "A perverse man spreads strife, and a slanderer separates intimate friends." (Proverbs 16:2)

God intends for no man to be without accountability. Pray that the board who oversees this leader will have the guts to confront him when he oversteps his bounds. If you are on a board that oversees this leader, then it is your job to seek to bring such a leader into line with what scripture teaches. In fact, it is the duty of such a board or a group of elders to make sure leaders do not overstep their scriptural bounds and lead in King Saul kinds of ways.

So go to the leader. If he won't hear you, go to the board that oversees him. If that does nothing then keep going to prayer, but don't go to war.

Jonathan even found the ability to stay under his father's leadership that he profoundly disagreed with. He went to battle with him. He respected the God given authority in his life. God may be asking you to learn from serving under a leader who is not yet as enlightened as you may think yourself to be. God often does this.

God may be freeing you to go somewhere else where you will be free to lead in a Jonathan type manner. But if you are attacking the place and the leaders that you left, then you are not a Jonathan type of leader at all. In fact, you are bitter, and please don't delude yourself by claiming some kind of righteous anger.

David learned from his mentor. Jonathan stood by his father even in death. And when God finally took Saul out of the game, David honored not only his friend Jonathan, but he honored King Saul in his profound commemorative lament.

> *Saul and Jonathan, beloved and pleasant in their*
> *life,*
> *And in their death they were not parted;*
> *They were swifter than eagles,*
> *They were stronger than lions.*
> *O daughters of Israel, weep over Saul,*
> *Who clothed you luxuriously in scarlet,*
> *Who put ornaments of gold on your apparel.*
> *How have the mighty fallen in the midst of the*
> *battle!*
> 2 Samuel 1:23-25

A Jonathan/David servant leader does not seek to destroy his own leaders but rather to influence and honor them to the best of his ability.

Following in Jonathan's Steps

This short book was written in hopes that leaders everywhere will see in themselves the natural tendencies to be just like King Saul, and in seeing this unwelcome truth would turn and desire to be like the Jonathan who gave the Kingdom away – to be like Jesus. But how can I change? What does a true servant leader look like?

A good friend and mentor to me, Marshall Christensen, teaches servant leadership principles all over the world. His colleague Dan Ballast has written a discussion guide to help churches, organizations, and businesses begin to change and grow into true servant leadership communities. This guide leads communities to discuss and live out what they have identified as 16 key principles of servant leadership communities. Through practicing these principles and living out these principles in community, King Saul will be put to rest and the Spirit that drove

Jonathan, Jesus, and the Apostle Paul will no longer be quenched, but be free to do his beautiful work.

Sixteen Principles of Servant Leadership

Community - Biblical leadership is not about pretending or coming across as knowing it all, but instead it is about coming together in community to seek truth through a process of action and reflection.

Values – The servant leader adopts values that reflect the supreme value of their relationship with God and people.

Influence – We influence by valuing the other person, building a relationship with them that brings light and life into their lives.

Integrity – These leaders are open, vulnerable, and transparent about their struggles and are quick to ask forgiveness. They develop influence by backing up their values with action.

Change – We are to influence by allowing the change that needs to take place in ourselves to indeed take place. We need to be seen actively changing into the core values we espouse.

Respect – We need to respect people not for what they have to offer us or based on some list of criteria, but simply because they are people.

Brokenness – Servant leaders greatly value others not only for their strengths but also for their areas of brokenness. We are to not hide our weakness and brokenness but are asked to minister through it, knowing it is the open door into others lives.

Sacrifice – We are asked to give up fame, position, power or gain so that others may be built up, knowing what is eternally gained far outweighs any temporary loss.

Listening – We are to give our time to be with others not simply to advance a corporate or personal agenda, but simply "to be" with others, listening to them and working to understand them.

Empathy – The actions of empathy go beyond listening as they involve further actions and time to gain an understanding of what it means to walk in another's shoes.

Service – Servant leaders think about how to meet the needs and serve others – both inside and outside their community – who are the neediest.

Purpose – Servant leaders help others discover and live their God given calling in the light of their own giftedness and brokenness so that they too may serve others

Acceptance – Servant leaders create open, honest and transparent "no-condemnation zones," so that people do not have to take up masks in order to function in the community.

Forgiveness – We must be willing to give and sacrifice in order to preserve relationships. This means extending the hand of forgiveness and offering restoration.

Empowering – We are to be constantly giving away the power God has given us. This means providing the resources and training to help others become even greater than ourselves.

Hard Work – Servant leadership requires taking difficult and humbling actions in the face of rejection, criticism, and doubts. It is about taking the narrow and often precarious path Jesus calls us to. And it is only in his example and strength we can prevail.

Any community growing in and living out these principles cannot be stopped for such is the Kingdom: it will not be stopped. I have had the privilege to see businesses – from apple orchards to high tech firms – and ministries – from churches to homeless shelters – all being transformed by the kind of leadership Jesus calls us to.

The "Building Servant Leadership Communities Discussion Guide" can be found at: <u>co-serve.org</u>. Please take the next step.

Epilogue

On a recent trip to Africa, I had the amazing opportunity to teach and be taught by a group of pastors and leaders in Karamoja, Uganda. As I was teaching the "Jonathan" servant leadership principles, one of the older pastors raised his hands and said this: "None of us would get angry or mad if our own son surpassed us in our giftings or achievements. We would be proud. So too we must be with those we serve. We should feel the delight of a father should one of our own disciples surpass us."

I reflected a moment on what he said. If my own son broke my high school track records (If I held any), I would rejoice. I would not be upset. In fact, it would be great even if my daughter beat my old records.

We are all members of one family. One body. One holy Church.

Each of the pastors, including the Bishop enthusiastically signed the following manifesto:

The Jonathan / David Manifesto

By God's power and the grace He alone gives…

I will train the people to do the work of the ministry rather than insisting on doing it myself or building it around myself. I will seek to empower and equip rather than to command and control. (See Ephesians 4:9-12)

I will seek to build God's big Kingdom in unison with other churches and pastors by praying for and working with them and I will not seek to build my own little kingdom. (See Matthew 6:33)

I will give thanks when I see others gifted like I am, and I will give them opportunities to exercise these gifts even if they should surpass my own. Instead of being threatened by them, I will build into them and let God use them, and teach them to do the same. (See Acts 18:24-28)

I will rejoice when God is working greatly through another pastor near me and will not allow it to make me jealous. (See Philippians 1:18)

I will wait on God to elevate me in position, by respecting those in leadership above me, and I will not seek to elevate myself my own way. (See Luke 14:7-11)

After signing the manifesto, in an amazing demonstration of transparency and obedience, the Bishop stood up and publically apologized to a young man 15 years younger than him for being insensitive to his needs as a young pastor when he had recently undergone some real hardship. He pledged to be a servant leader. The other pastors present were amazed by the humility of their leader. Apologies of leaders toward those under them are hardly heard in this part, or for that matter, any part of the world.

King Saul had just died. The syndrome was gone. It was replaced by the spirits and attitudes of Jonathan, John the Baptist, Jesus, and Paul. May the leadership they lived and died for – live in us. May Jesus live in and empower us.

It is time to get to work. It is time to serve. It is time to let go of the crown, give ourselves and our earthly kingdoms away, so we can advance the Kingdom of Heaven.

To purchase multiple copies of

Breaking the King Saul Syndrome,

please contact Co-Serve International at e-mail:

info@co-serve.org